Ramona Wood

Now Caitlin Can

A donated organ helps a child get well.

Abc Press
El Dorado, AR

To Mark Pinckard,
Who was giving in death as in life.
And to his family who allowed him to live on in others.

Printed in USA
Library of Congress Control Number: 2004094612

Wood, Ramona, 1957—
Now Caitlin can; a donated organ helps a child get well / by Ramona Wood;
illustrated by Ramona Wood—El Dorado, AR: Abc Press, 2004.
p. cm.
Summary: Freddie learns his little sister Caitlin's only chance for a
normal life is a kidney transplant. In time, a suitable kidney is donated
and Caitlin undergoes the surgery that changes her life.

ISBN 0-9758622-0-0

Freddie's baby sister Caitlin was *always* going to the hospital. When Caitlin was only four days old, she flew off in a helicopter for an operation.

And when they brought Caitlin home, she was *still* sick.

Freddie Pendzinski was upset. Would this little sister ever be the playmate that Mom and Dad promised?

Once Caitlin went to the hospital and got a tummy opening like the air hole on a beach ball.

After that, Mom fed Caitlin's formula straight into her tummy tube.

This new way of eating helped her to stop throwing up.

Freddie was sure glad *he* could eat the regular way.

Six-year-old Freddie asked what made Caitlin so sick.

"Caitlin's kidneys don't work right." Caitlin's doctor explained. "Kidneys are organs that usually clean waste products from our bodies. Caitlin can't tinkle wastes out like we do, so she has problems."

Freddie prayed for Caitlin every morning
on the way to school.

In the afternoon he ran through the
house till he found her. "Oh good!" he said.
"You're okay!"

Caitlin came home from the hospital *another* time with a dialysis tube in her side.

"What's di-a-ly-sis?" asked Freddie, "And why does she have that tail?"

"Come watch," Mom said. "We'll fasten Caitlin's 'monkey-tail' to her new dialysis machine. After a while, it drains the wastes from her body. This should help her."

The machine made a loud THUMP. Freddie ran off to watch TV with Dad.

Even with dialysis every night, Caitlin still had problems.

"What could *really* help my sister?" Freddie asked her doctor.

"When she's three years old, and weighs thirty-five pounds," said the doctor, "she might be able to get a kidney transplant."

"What's that?" asked Freddie.

"That's when someone donates, or gives a healthy kidney to someone whose kidneys don't work—like Caitlin."

It all sounded pretty strange. All Freddie knew was Caitlin needed something she couldn't have for a *really* long time.

Now and then, Caitlin felt okay so they went outside to play with the neighbor kids.

Caitlin studied her little friend. "Where is *your* monkey-tail?"

In the summer, Freddie had to sneak away to go swimming since Caitlin couldn't go in the water.

"If her tubes get wet," said Dad, "she could get an infection and get *really* sick."

Even the bathtub was off-limits for Caitlin. Mom wiped her clean with a sponge at bath time.

Caitlin got infections sometimes, no matter what.
One day they rushed her to the hospital with a very high fever.
A nurse said, "Wait here. There's nothing you can do."
But Freddie knew something he could do.
He prayed with all his heart: "God, Caitlin
needs help FAST!"

Caitlin's fever dropped suddenly and everyone was surprised—except Freddie.

"You better stay well now, if you want to get a kidney," he told her.

Finally Caitlin reached her third birthday.

"Hurray! You're old enough for a transplant," shouted Freddie.

"Now let's see if you weigh enough," said Dad.

Freddie saw she had a ways to go. He wished he could fatten her up with a pizza, but formula was all she could have.

"Not again!" said Caitlin every day when Freddie put her on the scales.

"You're getting closer, but you're not there yet," he would say.

Finally Caitlin weighed thirty-five pounds!

"Now can I get a new kidney?" Caitlin asked.

"First we'll call the hospital and get you on the waiting list," said Dad.

"Then they'll call us when the right kidney is ready," said Mom. "Since we're three hours from the hospital and a kidney must be transplanted quickly—let's go ahead and pack now."

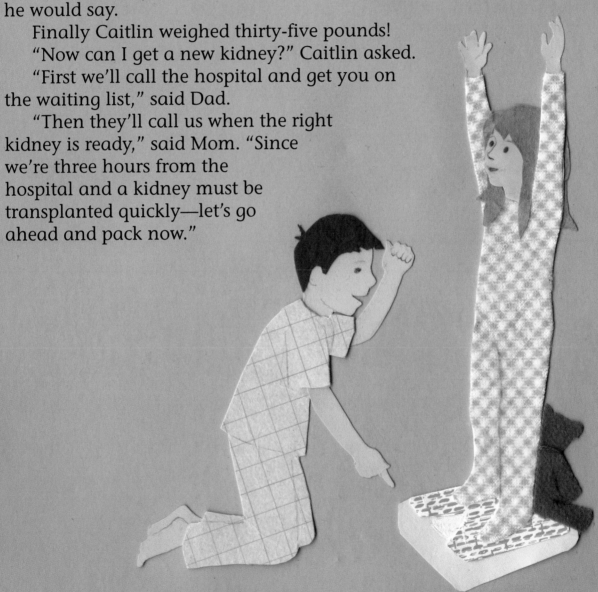

"No need to rush too much," said Dad. "Many people are ahead of Caitlin on the waiting list. So it could be a long time before she's given a kidney."

"Where do they get kidneys to transplant, anyway?" asked Freddie.

"Well, *sometimes* a living family member or friend will have surgery and give one of theirs," said Mom. "Since people have two, they recover and do fine with the other one. But the doctor said none of us were a good match for Caitlin."

"Other times," said Dad, "a kidney is a gift from someone—probably a stranger—who dies in an accident. That person's family says, 'Our loved one can't use his organs anymore. We hope they can help somebody else.'"

"Those people will be Caitlin's heroes!" said Freddie, "And they don't even know it."

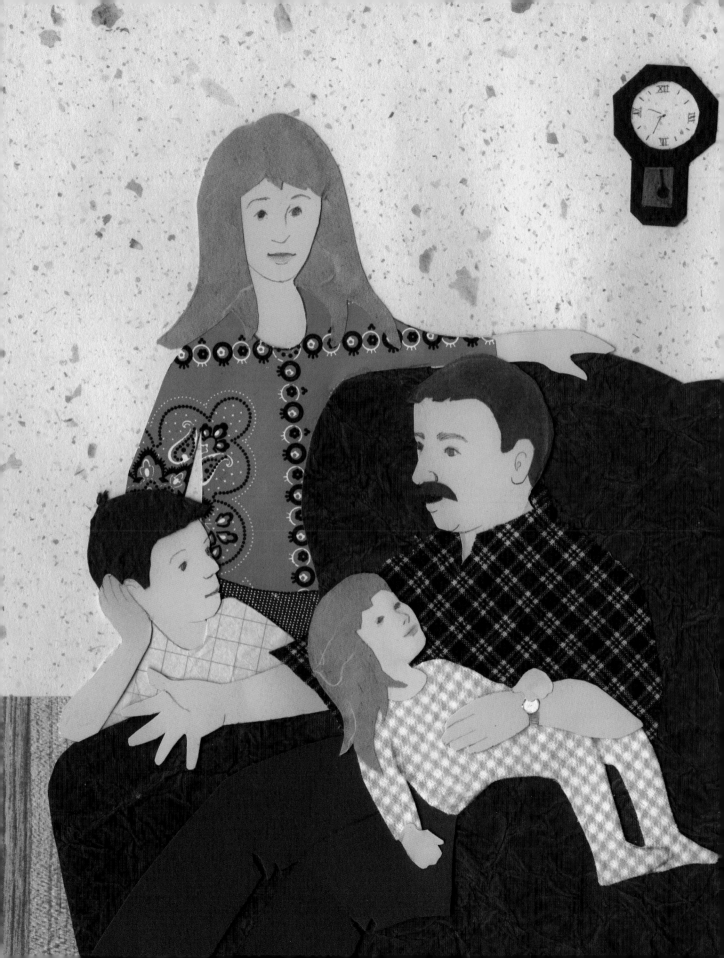

Caitlin often didn't feel well as the days and weeks passed.

At Thanksgiving the family thanked God for the people who helped whenever Caitlin was sick—friends, family and all the people at the hospital.

They also prayed for the people who would some day give Caitlin a kidney—and a new life.

The New Year brought lots of snow to play in, but Caitlin wasn't always up to playing.

"Race you to the tree!" Freddie shouted. Caitlin ran out of energy, but Freddie let her win anyway.

Caitlin turned four in the spring.

She closed her eyes and whispered, "I wish I could be well like everybody else."

Freddie helped her blow out the candles.

A few days after Caitlin's birthday, the telephone rang.
"Come quickly!" said the lady at the hospital. "There's a kidney for Caitlin."

Mom, Dad, Freddie and Caitlin raced out the door and headed to the hospital.

On the way, a siren screamed
from behind.

A police car with flashing blue lights
sped after them. Dad pulled over to the side
of the road.

"Do you know how fast you were driving?"
asked the policeman.

Freddie called from the back seat, "We *got* to
go *fast* for Caitlin's transplant! It's her only
chance to get well."

"Oh," said the policeman, "I see."
He radioed the next town: "Civilian car to
hospital at full speed. Send 'em through!"

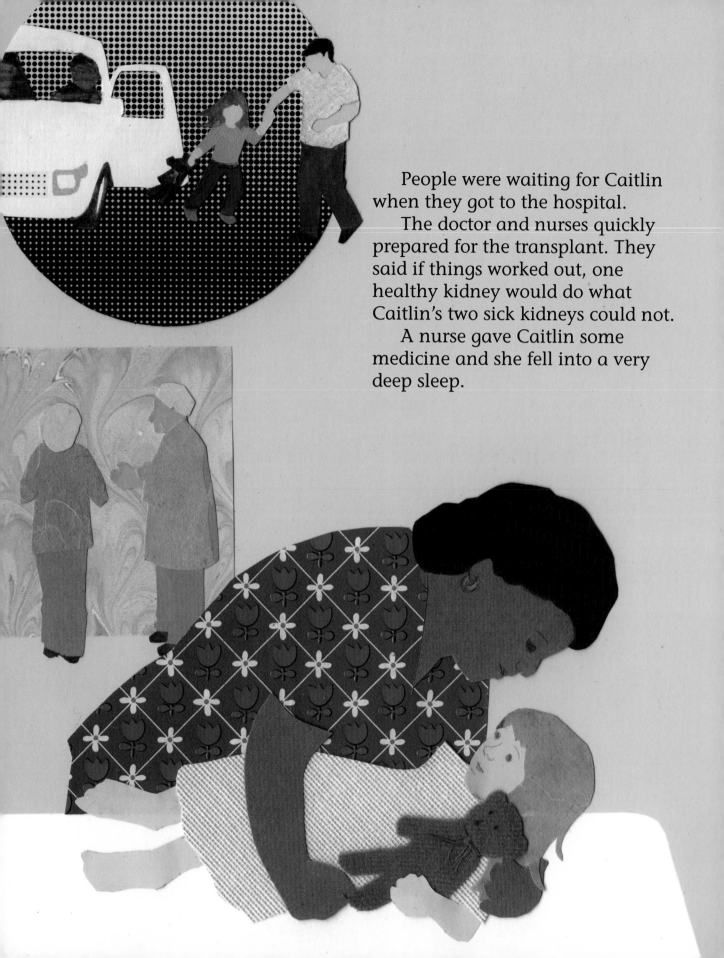

People were waiting for Caitlin when they got to the hospital.

The doctor and nurses quickly prepared for the transplant. They said if things worked out, one healthy kidney would do what Caitlin's two sick kidneys could not.

A nurse gave Caitlin some medicine and she fell into a very deep sleep.

Freddie heard the kidney for Caitlin came from a teenage donor named Mark. He died in a traffic accident.

Mark's friends heard him say once, if anything ever happened to him, he wanted his organs to go to anybody who needed them.

Mark's parents were very sad to lose their son. But they hoped part of Mark could help Caitlin.

Freddie prayed for Mark's family. He also prayed his sister would be all right.

Accident claims life of Teen

During the operation, Freddie and his parents waited for what seemed like forever.

Finally the doctor came out. He told them the surgery went fine. "But time will tell," he said, "if the kidney will keep on working."

When Freddie got to peek in, all Caitlin said was "Owee."
Then she rolled over.
Freddie worried. She didn't seem to be any better at all.
Mom said sometimes things seem worse before they get better.

Little by little Caitlin *did* get better. The next time Freddie saw her, she sat up in bed and said, "I'm hungry." When her food tray came, Caitlin started eating and didn't stop till she ran out of food.

"Now Caitlin can eat!" Freddie shouted, "And she needs some MORE."

One day a nurse helped Caitlin walk to the next room.

"Now Caitlin can go to the bathroom!" Freddie said.

"That proves the kidney's working," the doctor said, "In fact, Caitlin can go home now."

The doctor told them not to forget any of Caitlin's medicine. "And come back for checkups. We want to make sure she keeps on doing well."

Month after month went by and Caitlin got stronger every day.

At her fifth birthday party, she did a lot more than blow out the candles…

Caitlin got to *eat* cake and go swimming. She even won a race without Freddie letting her.

At the end of the day Caitlin prayed: "God, remember to thank the people who gave me a kidney and helped me feel better. And thank *you* for the best birthday I ever had."

Because of Mark's generous spirit, Caitlin's story has a happy ending.

On July 17, 2002, Caitlin Pendzinski met the family of the accident victim whose kidney made a world of difference in her life.

Left: Donor Mark Pinckard, ten days before his accident. Center photo from left: Phil (Mark's father), Caitlin, age four, Fred (Caitlin's father), Tina (Caitlin's mother), Heather (Mark's sister), and Jodie (Mark's mother). The Pendzinski's met the Pinckard family at ARORA—the Arkansas Regional Organ Recovery Agency in Little Rock. Right: Freddie at age six and his sister Caitlin, one, several years before the transplant.

In the U.S. alone, over 85,000 people are now waiting for the organs that could help them recover. About 17 people die every day because they don't receive the organs they need. If more families gave permission to donate their deceased loved one's organs, many more lives could be saved. Because Mark's family followed through with their son's wishes, Caitlin and four other people received the organs they desperately needed.

In many cases, family members are unaware of their loved one's desire to share their organs and fail to give this vital consent. You can help by discussing your wish to be a donor in the event of your death. For more information, go to www.donatelife.net or call the Coalition on Donation at 1-800-355-7427.

AUTHOR: Ramona Wood writes and illustrates stories about people in unusual situations. Her earlier book *The Goat Woman of Smackover* is about a folk-figure who lived in a circus truck for over fifty years. Visit www.saac-arts.org/rwood for more information.